The Last Ballad & Other Poems by John Davidson

John Davidson was born at Barrhead, East Renfrewshire on 11th April 1857.

In 1862 his family moved to Greenock and there he began his education at Highlanders' Academy. Davidson would now spend many years at school and the beginnings of a career in various industries before gaining employment in various schools.

By now literature was a large part of his activities and his first published work was 'Bruce, A Chronicle Play' in 1886. Four other plays quickly followed including the somewhat brilliant pantomimic 'Scaramouch in Naxos' (1889).

With his reputation gradually providing an income he was also able to explore his true medium; Verse. 'In a Music Hall and Other Poems' (1891) together with 'Fleet Street Eclogues' (1893) were ample proof that he possessed a quite rare, genuine and distinctive poetic gift.

Davidson now turned further and further towards verse. In 1894 he published his most popular volume, 'Ballads and Songs' (1894), and this was followed by a further 'Fleet Street Eclogues' (Second Series) (1896) and by 'New Ballads' (1897) and 'The Last Ballad' (1899).

As the new century dawned Davidson was hard at work on a series of 'Testaments', in which he gave definite expression to his philosophy and were published over a seven year period; 'The Testament of a Vivisector' (1901), 'The Testament of a Man Forbid' (1901), 'The Testament of an Empire Builder' (1902), and 'The Testament of John Davidson' (1908).

However, on 23rd March 1909, with his finances in ruins, the onset of cancer and profound hopelessness and clinical depression he left his house for the last time. His body was only found on September 18th by some local fishermen.

Index of Contents

THE LAST BALLAD

By coasts where scalding deserts reek,
The apanages of despair;
In outland wilds, by firth and creek,
O'er icy bournes of silver air;

In storm or calm delaying not,
To every noble task addressed,
Year after year, Sir Lancelot
Fulfilled King Arthur's high behest.

He helped the helpless ones; withstood
Tyrants and sanctioners of vice;
He rooted out the dragon brood,
And overthrew false deities.

Alone with his own soul, alone
With life and death, with day and night,
His thought and strength grew great and shone
A tongue of flame, a sword of light.

And yet not all alone. On high,
When midnight set the spaces free,

And brimming stars hung from the sky
Low down, and spilt their jewellery.

Behind the nightly squandered fire.
Through a dark lattice only seen
By love, a look of rapt desire
Fell from a vision of the Queen.

From heaven she bent when twilight knit
The dusky air and earth in one;
He saw her like a goddess sit
Enthroned upon the noonday sun.

In passages of gulfs and sounds,
When wild winds dug the sailor's grave,
When clouds and billows merged their bounds,
And the keel climbed the slippery wave,

A sweet sigh laced the tempest; nay,
Low at his ear he heard her speak;
Among the hurtling sheaves of spray
Her loosened tresses swept his cheek.

And in the revelry of death.
If human greed of slaughter cast
Remorse aside, a violet breath,
The incense of her being passed

Across his soul, and deeply swayed
The fount of pity; o'er the strife
He curbed the lightning of his blade.
And gave the foe his forfeit life.

Low on the heath, or on the deck,
In bloody mail or wet with brine.
Asleep he saw about her neck
The wreath of gold and rubies shine;

He saw her brows, her lovelit face,
And on her cheek one passionate tear;
He felt in dreams the rich embrace.
The beating heart of Guinevere.

"Visions that haunt my couch, my path,
Although the waste, unfathomed sea
Should rise against me white with wrath
I must behold her verily,

"Once ere I die," he said, and turned
Westward his faded silken sails
From isles where cloudy mountains burned,
And north to Severn-watered Wales.

Beside the Usk King Arthur kept
His Easter court, a glittering rout.
But Lancelot, because there swept
A passion of despair throughout

His being, when he saw once more
The sky that canopied, the tide
That girdled Guinevere, forbore
His soul's desire, and wandered wide

In unknown seas companionless.
Eating his heart, until by chance
He drifted into Lyonesse,
The wave-worn kingdom of romance.

He leapt ashore and watched his barque
Unmastered stagger to its doom;
Then doffed his arms and fled baresark
Into the forest's beckoning gloom.

The exceeding anguish of his mind
Had broken him. "King Arthur's trust,"
He cried; "ignoble, fateful, blind!
Her love and my love, noxious lust!

"Dupes of our senses! Let us eat
In caverns fathoms underground,
Alone, ashamed! To sit at meat
In jocund throngs? — the most profound

"Device of life the mountebank,
Vendor of gilded ashes! Steal
From every sight to use the rank
And loathsome needs that men conceal;

"And crush and drain in curtained beds
The clusters called of love; but feed
With garlanded uplifted heads;
Invite the powers that sanction greed

"To countenance the revel; boast
Of hunger, thirst; be drunken; claim
Indulgence to the uttermost,

Replenishing the founts of shame!"

He gathered berries, efts, and snails,
Sorrel, and new-burst hawthorn leaves;
Uprooted with his savage nails
Earth-nuts; and under rocky eaves

Shamefast devoured them, out of sight
In darkness, lest the eye of beast.
Or bird, or star, or thing of night
Uncouth, unknown, should watch him feast.

At noon in twilight depths of pine
He heard the word Amaimon spoke;
He saw the pallid, evil sign
The wred-eld lit upon the oak.

The viper loitered in his way;
The minx looked up with bloodshot leer;
Ill-meaning fauns and lamiæ
With icy laughter flitted near.

But if he came upon a ring
Of sinless elves, and crept unseen
Beneath the brake to hear them sing.
And watch them dancing on the green,

They touched earth with their finger-tips;
They ceased their roundelay; they laid
A seal upon their elfin lips
And vanished in the purple shade.

At times he rent the dappled flank
Of some fair creature of the chase,
Mumbled its flesh, or growling drank
From the still-beating heart, his face

And jowl ruddled, and in his hair
And beard, blood-painted straws and burs,
While eagles barked screening the air.
And wolves that were his pensioners.

Sometimes at night his mournful cry
Troubled all waking things; the mole
Dived to his deepest gallery;
The vixen from the moonlit knoll

Passed like a shadow underground,

And the mad satyr in his lair
Whined bodeful at the world-old sound
Of inarticulate despair.

Sir Lancelot, beloved of men!
The ancient earth gat hold of him;
A year was blotted from his ken
In the enchanted forest dim.

At Easter when the thorn beset
The bronzing wood with silver sprays,
And hyacinth and violet
Empurpled all the russet ways;

When buttercup and daffodil
A stainless treasure-trove unrolled.
And cowslips had begun to fill
Their chalices with sweeter gold,

He heard a sound of summer rush
By swarthy grove and kindled lawn;
He heard, he sighed to hear the thrush
Singing alone before the dawn.

Forward he stalked with eyes on fire
Like one who keeps in sound and sight
An angel with celestial lyre
Descanting rapturous delight.

He left behind the spell-bound wood;
He saw the branchless air unfurled;
He climbed a hill and trembling stood
Above the prospect of the world.

With lustre in its bosom pent
From many a shining summer day
And harvest moon, the wan sea leant
Against a heaven of iron-grey.

Inland on the horizon beat
And flickered, drooping heavily,
A fervid haze, a vaporous heat,
The dusky eyelid of the sky.

White ways, white gables, russet thatch
Fretted the green and purple plain;
The herd undid his woven latch;
The bleating flock went forth again;

The skylarks uttered lauds and prime;
The sheep-bells rang from hill to hill;
The cuckoo pealed his mellow chime;
The orient bore a burden shrill.

His memory struggled half awake;
Dimly he groped within to see
What star, what sun, what light should break
And set his darkened spirit free.

But from without deliverance came:
Afar he saw a horseman speed,
A knight, a spirit clad in flame
Riding upon a milk-white steed.

For now the sun had quenched outright
The clouds and all their working charms.
Marshalled his legionary light.
And fired the rider's golden arms.

Softly the silver billows flowed;
Beneath the hill the emerald vale
Dipped seaward; on the burnished road
The milk-white steed, the dazzling mail

Advanced and flamed against the wind;
And Lancelot, his body rent
With the fierce trial of his mind
To know, reeled down the steep descent.

Remembrances of battle plied
His soul with ruddy beams of day.
"A horse! a lance! to arms!" he cried,
And stood there weeping in the way.

"Speak!" said the knight. "What man are you?"
"I know not yet. Surely of old
I rode in arms, and fought and slew
In jousts and battles manifold."

Oh, wistfully he drew anear,
Fingered the reins, the jewelled sheath;
With rigid hand he grasped the spear.
And shuddering whispered, " Life and death,

"Love, lofty deeds, renown — did these
Attend me once in days unknown?"

With courtesy, with comely ease.
And brows that like his armour shone,

The golden knight dismounting took
Sir Lancelot by the hand and said,
"Your voice of woe, your lonely look
As of a dead man whom the dead

"Themselves cast out — whence are they, friend?"
Sir Lancelot a moment hung
In doubt, then knelt and made an end
Of all his madness, tensely strung

In one last effort to be free
Of evil things that wait for men
In secret, strangle memory,
And shut the soul up in their den.

"Spirit," he said, "I know your eyes:
They bridge with light the heavy drift
Of years.... A woman said, "Arise;
And if you love the Queen, be swift!"

"The token was an emerald chased
In gold, once mine. Wherefore I rode
At dead of night in proudest haste
To Payarne where the Queen abode.

"A crafty witch gave me to drink:
Almost till undern of the mom
Silent, in darkness. . . . When I think
It was not Guinevere, self-scorn

"Cuts to the marrow of my bones,
A blade of fire. Can wisdom yield
No moody no counsel, that atones
For wasted love! . . . Heaven had revealed

"That she should bear a child to me
My bed-mate said. . . . Yet am I mad?
The offspring of that treachery!
The maiden knight! You — Galahad,

"My son, who make my trespass dear!"
His look released his father's thought —
The darkling orbs of Guinevere;
For so had Lancelot's passion wrought.

With tenderer tears than women shed
Sir Galahad held his father fast.
"Now I shall be your squire," he said.
But Lancelot fought him long. At last

The maiden gently overpowered
The man. Upon his milk-white steed
He brought him where a castle towered
Midmost a green enamelled mead;

And clothed his body, clothed his heart
In human garniture once more.
"My father, bid me now depart.
I hear beside the clanging shore,

"Above the storm, or in the wind,
Outland, or on the old Roman street,
A chord of music intertwined
From wandering tones deep-hued and sweet.

"Afar or near, at noon, at night,
The braided sound attends and fills
My soul with peace, as heaven with light
O'erflows when morning crowns the hills.

"And with the music, seen or hid,
A blood-rose on the palace lawn,
A fount of crimson, dark amid
The stains and glories of the dawn;

"Above the city's earthly hell
A token ominous of doom,
A cup on fire and terrible
With thunders in its ruddy womb;

"But o'er the hamlet's fragrant smoke.
The dance and song at eventide,
A beating heart, the gentle yoke
Of life the bridegroom gives the bride;

A ruby shadow on the snow;
A flower, a lamp — through every veil
And mutable device I know,
And follow still the Holy Grail

"Until God gives me my new name
Empyreal, and the quest be done.
Then like a spirit clad in flame.

He kissed his father and was gone.

Long gazed Sir Lancelot on the ground
Tormented till benign repose
Enveloped him in depths profound
Of sweet oblivion. When he rose

The bitterest was past. "And I
Shall follow now the Holy Grail,
Seen, or unseen, until I die:
My very purpose shall avail

"My soul," he said. By day, by night,
He rode abroad, his vizor up;
With sun and moon his vehement sight
Fought for a vision of the cup —

In vain. For evermore on high
When darkness set the spaces free.
And brimming stars hung from the sky
Low down, and spilt their jewellery,

Behind the nightly squandered fire.
Through a dim lattice only seen
By love, a look of rapt desire
Fell from a vision of the Queen.

From heaven she bent when twilight knit
The dusky air and earth in one;
He saw her like a goddess sit
Enthroned upon the noonday sun.

Wherefore he girt himself again:
In lawless towns and savage lands.
He overthrew unrighteous men,
Accomplishing the King's commands.

In passages of gulfs and sounds
When wild winds dug the sailor's grave,
When clouds and billows merged their bounds,
And the keel climbed the slippery wave,

A sweet sigh laced the tempest; nay.
Low at his ear he heard her speak;
Among the hurtling sheaves of spray
Her loosened tresses swept his cheek.

And in the revelry of death.

If human greed of slaughter cast
Remorse aside, a violet breath,
The incense of her bring passed

Across his soul, and deeply swayed
The fount of pity; o'er the strife
He curbed the lightning of his blade.
And gave the foe his forfeit life.

His love, in utter woe annealed.
Escaped the furnace, sweet and clear-
His love that on the world had sealed
The look, the soul of Guinevere.

THE ORDEAL

Exceedingly tame is the devil, with all his forks and flaming stuff:
To be conscious and not omnipotent is more than torture enough.

Between the Golden City and the sea
A damasked meadow lay, the saffron beach
And silver loops of surge dissevering
The violet water from the grass-green land.

While yet the morning sun swung low in heaven,
A crystal censer in a turquoise dome,
Emanuel meted justice in the gate,
Emanuel of the Golden City King.

To him there came Sir Hilary; his wife,
The comely Bertha; after them their sons
And daughters grieving. Godfrey also came,
Knight-errant of the Phoenix; from that quest
Lately returned: guarded he was and bound.

"Justice, my lord and king!" cried Hilary,
With passion hoarse, and wanner than a flame
That flickers in the sun. "I saw them kiss:
I saw her from her bosom take a ring
And place it warm upon his finger. Here" —
He gave the King the ring — "an old worn hoop
Of pale alloy, but clasping, doubt it not,
Shorde of sweet and shameful memories
More dear to them than mines of virgin gold.
Justice, my lord and king!"

"Whom do you charge?"

"Sir Godfrey and my wife. I saw them kiss;
I saw her tearfully assign the ring
Warm from her bosom to his lustful hand.
For him the gallows and for her the stake!"

"But if you saw this done, Sir Hilary,
Why is her lover here alive to-day?"

"I ran upon him in the garden-close
When I espied them; but he beat me back.
Hearing the clash of steel my folk rushed forth
And fettered him. Vengeance miscarrying thus,
Before the world the law shall have its way.
The age is dissolute; the hearts of men
Allow every sin by rote; their starveling souls
The blind and lame: I publish my disgrace
And warn the world. This woman is my wife;
These well-grown youths; these budding damsels — look . . .
I scarce can say the words . . . look you, my liege,
These are our children: treasure, you would say,
To fill a woman's heart? Oh no! He there,
That lecher, is her lover, gray and gaunt.

If she be burned before her children's eyes,
The wanton blood they have from her, refined
By fire, in her fierce torment drained and seared,
May leave them humble-hearted and afraid
Even of the lawful kiss of married love.
Justice, my lord, upon the shameful pair!"
"Do they admit the charge? What do you say,
Sir Godfrey? Bertha, answer."

"All my life,"
The lady said, looking upon the ground:
Because when she looked up her stricken eyes
Turned to her children, sorrowing by her side;
And her true heart when most she needed strength
Began to break: wherefore upon the ground
She cast her gaze and answered, "All my life
I have been faithful to my husband's bed."

"And I," said Godfrey, "never did him wrong."

Knight-errant of the Phoenix, fancy-charmed
At fifty still, but as inept to lie
As tongueless men to sing, even furtive minds

A grudging credence paid him: jealousy
That calls the moon a leper, and will swear
There never was a maid of sweet sixteen,
Only the heart's attorney, jealousy.
Had any countenance to doubt his word.

"He lies," cried Hilary, "as their lovers' code
Requires."

The ring, the keepsake?" said the King:
Did you receive it with a kiss from her?"
"I kissed her, and she gave me back the ring."

"Oh! she returned the ring!" cried Hilary.
"A stale, old shame! I might have guessed as much.
The happiest of men I judged myself.
My wife, so delicate, so meek, so chaste,
A rare obedience gave; but unperfumed,
Unlit by passion: so she seemed, and so
To me she was, because her false blood burned
In the dark-lantern of a lawless love,
Where did be hunt the Phoenix? Ask him that.
How often has he, wandering secretly,
Discovered in my arbours, here at home,
Or on my pillows, Araby the Blest?"

"Nay," said the King; "have patience, Hilary.
Godfrey plead; she after him shall tell
own romance. Lead her aside meanwhile."

"Content," said Hilary.

And it was done.
Her children gathered round her as she went,
Worship and sorrow fighting in their looks.
The youngest, eager to be near her, trod
Upon her skirt, making her halt. Abashed
He shrank behind the others; but she turned,
Andy seeing him distressed, held out her hand.
Moving her fingers as she used to do
Winningly when her children first could walk.
She sent him also so humane a smile.
So sweet, so patient, that his ruddy cheek
Grew pale as hers; and, suffering more than she.
Because he hardly knew — and yet he knew—
The naked meaning of his father's charge,
He cried aloud, and, throttled by his sobs,
Sank to the ground: the mounting tide of life

Had but begun to press upon his heart
With murmured news of mystery unveiled;
And all his fancy innocently clung
About his mother — he, her latest born;
And she, his earliest sweetheart.

Silently,
Before another could, she reached her son,
And lifted him and bore him in her arms.
Dismayed to find himself a babe again,
He pushed her from him, straining towards the ground.
"Be still!" she said. "This is a thing to do!
Something to do!" and crushed him to her breast.

East of the city wall a virgin wood
Discovered twilight gleams of emerald
In depths of leafy darkness treasured up.
Upon its verge a grove of hawthorn hung,
The friendly tree — and Nature's favourite:
For now that all its own unhoarded bloom
Was withered, and its incense sacrificed,
The honeysuckle lit the matted boughs
With cressets burning odour, and the briar
Enwreathed and overhung them lovingly,
Its pallid rose like elfin faces sweet
Peering from out the swart-green thicket side.

Thither they led dame Bertha. In the shade
She sat: her son, still as a nursling now,
With solemn eyes where stately dreams reside.
Lay in her arms and watched her ashen lips.
The brilliant blackbirds, sauntering through the brake,
Doled out indifferently their golden notes.
Or sprinkled magic phrases, summer showers
Of jewelled rain, the while Sir Godfrey's voice
Re-echoed faintly from the City gate.
Then Bertha, all benumbed with misery.
Caressed her son, and, swaying to and fro.
In troubled whispers told a fairy tale
Of how a lady, deeply wronged, became
The happiest princess in the world at last.
Her other children, kneeling by her side.
Powerless to comfort, worshipped her and wept.

Sir Godfrey, standing bound before the King,
Spoke thus: "My cognizance has wrought my fate:
A Phoenix burning in his nest; the scroll,
Viget in cinere virtus. In my youth

I swore to find the Phoenix, being scorned
By many who averred that no such fowl
Inhabited the earth. And here, my lord,
Before I answer Hilary's reproach,
I beg all men to know the Phoenix lives;
For I have seen him fly across the Nile,
Beating the air with gold and purple plumes,
Towards Yemen, where he reigns: this was last year,
The thirtieth of my quest."

"Sir," said the King:
"I marvel at your patience. Thirty years!"
"Patience? I know it not! Embarked, I swore
That thirty weeks, and sorely grudged the time,
Should see the Phoenix caught and caged; myself,
Renowned throughout the world, and fixed in fame
With Lancelot and Roland. Youth and hope
Spare none of us — Syren and Circe linked
In one divine betrayal of the world!
Even while the Golden City towered behind
And bathed its glittering shadow in the deep
The Berber galleys swooped: captivity
Her twisted talons settled in my flesh
To tire on body and soul with dripping beak
For thrice the time I vowed. That was the dawn!

Also in Hadramaut, five savage years
Of lash and shackle, scornful destiny
Awarded me. Tenacious death, in shapes
Of thraldom, pestilence, contention, thirst,
Shipwreck and famine, flame and blind despair,
Remained my mate by day, my watch by night.
Yet, and although I still am buffeted
By every busy wind and stroke of chance:
Deceived, disgraced, contemptuously foiled
By oracles, by wantonness of fools.
And by the sleepless masked malignity
That men pursue the soul of man withal,
I am neither taught nor tamed. Intolerance
Of mundane things — of utter sanctity
As of indulged desire — shines in the stars,
And in the icy menace of the moon.

From them my fire is kindled, keenest flame
Of passion; for I look not to be praised
Here in the courts of Kings and homes of men;
Nor happily hereafter to usurp
A blissful throne of that imagined world

By terror-stricken envy reared in air
For the immortal solace and reward
Of humbleness and chastity, the true
Accomplices, the virtuous other selves
Of mediocrity and impotence.
But I desire to follow out this quest:
Achieved or unachieved it is my own:
Even if the glorious creature were no more. . . .
A foolish word! I have seen him, as I said:
From Heliopolis he took his flight

Towards Yemen, like a rainbow laced with gems.
Whether I find him, or am overthrown
Pursuing him, the world shall never know:
My purpose is sufficient for my soul.
Farewell at once. I must be gone — again
To feel my heart leap at the sudden foe.
The lonely battle in the wilderness;
To come at night under the desert moon
On pillars, ghostly porches, temples, towers
Silent for centuries; to see at dawn
The shadow of the Arab on the sand."

Sir Godfrey bowed and strode a pace away;
Then stopped like one enchanted, wondering
What spell o'ermastered him. When from his dream
He woke, and felt his pinioned arms, a blush
Shone on his tawny cheek and untanned brow.
He muttered something quickly; stumbled — stood,
Staring before him.

"Mediocrity
And impotence!" cried Hilary. "The phrase,
The very motto lechery inscribes
Beneath the cuckold's sign armorial,
Crested dilemma, honour's hatchment, horns.
This Phoenix-hunt, this magpie-tale of his
Allures no sober judgment from the nest
He fouled! Incredible effrontery!"

"Not in my thought, Sir Hilary," said the King,
"I cannot press a finger on the wrist
Of treason, and declare 'This blood is false';
Nor is there a divining-rod for kings
To tell the hearts of gold; but I dare stake
My Crown against an apple that the man
Is honest: he forgot the charge preferred
Against him. — Answer me: How came you, sir.

To be discovered with Sir Hilary's wife?"

"Oh, very simply!" said Sir Godfrey.

"Ay!"
Groaned Hilary in his beard; "simply enough!"
"When I at last beheld the Phoenix, watched
His dazzling flight stream through the east- em air.
The sun fell down behind me, and my heart
Beset me in the darkness. Overpowered
By deep desire to repossess a ring
That was my mother's . . . Many men, my lord.
Of hardihood sufficient have been known
To hold the memories of their mothers dear
I told myself that having seen once more
The Golden City, wandered through its streets
Of cheerful folk, and by the windy wharfs
Where silent shipmen hang about, and stir
The hearts of passers strangely, never more
Should any thought withdraw me from my quest.
As for the ring, I knew not Hilary's wife
Possessed it; but I knew that Bertha did.
It happened thus: At twenty years, alone
And penniless, house, trinkets — all I sold
To furnish fame with wings; and straightway shipped
For Egypt and the Phoenix. Ere we sailed
I saw this Bertha wistfully approach.
And ran to her, for we were pleasant friends-
Sweethearts, perhaps. Younger than I she was,
And like a palm-tree tall and lithe. I think
Until that day I had not said one word
Of love; but in the morning, half in jest,
Shamefast I whispered, bidding her goodbye,
And will you marry me when I come back?"
Her blood dyed all her face and neck deep red:
She leaned aside and gazed askance with looks
As wide as day; then fronted me. Her sighs
Bat from her open mouth hot on my face
Like scented winds that blow in Hadramaut.
She trembled, sobbed, and while I wondered fled —
In anger or in love I could not tell."

"Ay, ay!" went Hilary, with the dog-like leer
Of one whose ribs are grilled by torturers.

"But when she sought me out upon the ship,
And silently embraced me meeting her,
I knew, I surely knew that it was love.

She knotted in my scarf a silken purse,
And said, ' A keepsake. Give me something, sir."
The ring, my lord, was all I had to give.
I would have pawned, as I have spent, my soul
To serve my purpose: that metallic lie.
My mother's talisman — its paltriness
As merchandise and unappraisable
Romance preserved it. Often I had watched
My mother turn and turn it lost in thought;
And watching I divined its history.
With hoarded pence, my father, straitly kept,
Had bought it for her on a festival
When they were children: love began with them
In April: and she showed me — for I asked
If I divined aright — half-hidden zones
Engraved as with her ripening the ring
On divers fingers had reposed in turn.
Quickly at Bertha's vehement desire
I offered the remembrance I had kept.
She stretched her hand — a fragrant lily hand.
And slipped a petal through the pinchbeck hoop;
Then clad me in her glance and stole away.

Now that I think, I never have beheld
In any other face or other eyes
Of man or woman, or hero in my dreams,
So great a passion, so profound a hope."

"Ha!" cried the King. "Regret has found you out?"

"Oh no, my lord! My spirit stands aloof
In judgment of the past. The Moorish whips
Cut from my fancy Bertha's image, pale
Even at the start. Scarcely, until I longed
To have my mother's ring, did any thought
Of Bertha's love offend me in my quest.
After delays — the lackeys circumstance
Provides abundantly for all my schemes—
I reached the Golden City. Hilary's wife,
They told me, was the Bertha I had known.
I found her house, and seeing her without —
It could be no one else; indeed I seemed
To catch her walk again — I went to her,
Withdrawn among a grove of cypresses.
And asked her headlong for my mother's ring.
She gave it me, as Hilary says, and looked.
Poor soul, so sad, that pity wrung my heart.
I kissed her brow: down fell the silvery tears,

And thrice she tried to speak; but Hilary came
And made this ugly rent in our adieus."

"This is the truth," said King Emanuel.

"Lies! Subtle lies!" the husband hissed.
"Hear her!
The trap he sets himself. If her account
Accord with his, chance deals in miracles."

Said Godfrey then, "My lord, I kissed his wife,
And therefore overlook the littleness
Of his attack; but now that he has heard
The truth, and still denies my honesty,
I claim the combat."

"And the claim is just,"
Emanuel said. "I stand for God; but step
Aside, well-pleased that He should arbitrate
Immediately. So, let the lists be set."

"But Bertha's story?" stammered Hilary.
"Sir," said the King. "The combat shall decide
Whether your wife requires to plead or no."

"Well— very well!" said Hilary. "I am old;
My joints are stiff; my sinews slack; my sight
Begins to fail; 'tis ebbtide in my blood:
He like a lion from the desert comes
Supple and strong with questing up and down.
Behold an opportunity for God —
Which He will profit by!"

"I doubt it not,"
The King said meaningly.

But Godfrey said,
"What prate is this? I am the better man.
And Hilary shall fall before my lance."
At noon the lists were set. About the earth.
Whose sea-enamelled disk resplendent wheeled
Among the hidden stars, deep-bosomed clouds,
Horizon-haunting, towered and stooped; the sun
Poured from his quenchless urn, high-held in heaven,
A silent cataract of light, whereto
The mounting larks with sinewy wings and throats
Of tempered gold harnessed a voice inspired.
But in the shining City the tilt-yard hummed

With the inhuman gossip of the world —
The lickerish crowd agape to dip their mouths
In purple-streaming agony, distrained
From hearts mature for torture, newly plucked
And cast into the press.

Emanuel,
Whenas the sullen-sounding bell had rung
The heavy peal of noon, gave forth the word.
Straightway the trumpets rang, and every look
Towards Bertha veered at once. The petulant throng
Again and yet again, with puckered brows
And hands aslant against the naked light,
Had prowled and peered, and launched surmises wide
Of her repose and countenance serene —
Inscrutable to eyes of cavillers;
But now the winepress flowed, the bout began
With winks and elbowings and nimble nods.
For at the trumpets' call a scarlet sign
Flashed up on Bertha's face; and from the post
Where opposite the King she stood alone.
Patient and proud, a smile of utter peace,
A shaft of glory on her children fell;
And they, disburdened, stretched their hands and laughed:
Since God Himself had hung His balance out,
Already they could hear the host of Heaven,
With psalteries and far-resounding songs,
Acclaim their mother's starry chastity,
And laud the righteous Judge of all the earth.

A second time the trumpets rang — a cry
Implacable with shrieking echoes winged;
Then silence like a heavy dew came down.
Before a breath could move the stagnant air.
And while the pennoned lances of the twain —
Godfrey and Hilary in arms of proof —
Upon the summons in the sockets couched
Still quivered pausing, overthwart the lists
A vagrant bee twanged like an airy lyre
Of one rich-hearted chord. Swift underneath
The honey-laden track the gleaming hoofs
Of either spur-wrung charger gripped the ground,
Flung forth and spanned the course with fluent speed
Of thudding leaps entwined. Together hurled
In uncontrolled assault — each rivet wrenched,
Each nerve and artery of horse and man
Shot through with scalding flame — helm-smitten, both
Hung overborne and toppling urgently,

Till Hilary in his stirrups rose and screamed.
Startling his mastered steed, "Go down to Hell"—
Astounded at his triumph and meanly glad
That Godfrey should have fallen pierced through the brain
By his haphazard, his unworthy lance,
"Go down to Hell, and cook your Phoenix there!"

The instant murmur of the tossing crowd
Sprang to a roar; and like a home-sick wretch
Delivered from the storm whose gliding hull
Founders upon the welcome harbour-bar,
The voice of malice thrust into her ears
Even as the din and hubbub of the sea
Deafens the drowning outcast, Bertha fell
Wrecked in the very haven of her hope.

Her children, led by him whom she had nursed
To cheat the time beneath the hawthorn-shade.
Tongue-tied with grief and dazzled by their tears,
But bright instinctive creatures in the speed
And promptness of their act, maidens and youths,
O'erskipped the barrier. Bertha then, sustained
By hands of love that trembled and were strong,
Arose, and midmost of her brood at bay
Confronted the eclipse of her renown.
His latticed vizor raised, Sir Hilary cried
Above the dwindled clamour, "Heaven has judged,
Oh King Emanuel! Bid her now confess!"

"I bid her speak. Speak, Bertha," said the King,
Heart-struck and pale, but waiting yet on God;
While all the quidnuncs inly hugged themselves.
And market-haunters chafed their sweaty palms.
For now, indeed, the winepress overflowed.

Heading her cygnets, Bertha paced the lists
Towards the throne, a stately sufferer.
Her courtesy not forgotten, and her glance
Sweeping the gazers till it lit and hung
Upon the watchful King; in either hand
A child's close-clasped; and in her bosom pent
A tide of tears, she stood till silence reigned
Then lifted up a sick and shuddering voice
But Hilary broke out, "What need, my lord?
The judgment has been given: the sentence now
Is all that should be said."

"Your best and word

Is said and done!" the King declared
"What should
And should not be, who dare assume? God's mind
Is not apparent yet. Your wife shall speak."

"Now, is this just? " said Hilary,

"Just?" she cried.
"My children at my skirt, before the world,
My zealous husband and the King and God,
I wish to speak! " Intolerant at last,
Her mouth distorted and her eyes on fire.
She threw her piercing challenge out: "My love
Was never Hilary's!" That said, she paused.
The mistress of her audience. Slowly then
She bent her gaze on Godfrey's mail-clad corpse:
Through the crushed beaver — the floodgate of his life —
A crimson current sluiced his helm, and stained
With ruddy umber a sodden patch of sand.
But steadfastly she looked and proudly spake:
"I loved the dead man there. O King, O God"—
Now to the earthly throne and now to heaven —
"His was the face and form adored the most
By noble maidens, grave and ardent: his
The highest heart, the freest soul of all
The aspirants of the City in the days
When love laid claim to us who now are old.
In dreams and potent melancholy steeped
I felt the subtile essence, the desire.
The pure, unmingled virtue of my life
Yield up itself, a suppliant passion, bound
To minister to his, or waste away
The impatient captive of his memory.

He loved me as a young man loves who knows
By hearsay only of the deeds of love —
As virgins love he loved me; but without
The overwhelming anguish I endured,
I being a woman. When at last he spoke
It was not till the luckless day he sailed
On his adventure: 'Would I marry him
When he came back?' My heart took fire: it seemed
To melt and flow: speech failed me and I fled.
But in the evening, when the land-breeze blew,
Breathless I hurried through the murmuring streets
Refreshed with scent of meadow-hay new-reaped
Behind the Golden City. He saw me come
Staring along the quay; he leapt ashore;

He kissed me: but the ropes were casting off;
The ripple beat and chid his tardy barque.
I twisted in his dress a silken purse
With twenty golden ducats of my own;
He on my finger thrust that piteous ring:
And straight the sundering ocean lay between,
All in the springtime thirty years ago."

"A perfect tale," cried Hilary. "A plot
Nicely prepared!"

"I have not done," she said.
"Love like a dragon breathing smoke and armed
In jewelled scales withdrew me to the den
Of starless night his burning orbs illume.
Whene'er I struggled in that dreadful hold,
Where only long-drawn sighs are heard and groans
Unpitied ever, adamantine fangs
Were mortised in my heart. So clutched and torn,
Year after year I waited on my knight.
My lover, to deliver me from love.
But madness came instead and death stood near:
These the abounding vigour of my race,
And youth, long-suffering, quickly over-powered.
Forthwith to blight my new-blown summer-time
The vision of my hero dawned once more,
And at my chamber-window in the night
I saw the jewelled dragon vigilant.
Then was it that I turned to thee, O God
Who madest me! 'Thy handmaid. Lord,'
I said;
'Pity Thy handmaid! Him whom I adore
On earth the most — in Thine own image shaped
More excellently than all men beside —
Has wandered over sea: no message comes,
No token; none report him; he is lost —
Is dead to me, for I am more than thought.
Must I descend into the dust again
And of my body see no fruit at all?
O God, the heaped-up treasure of delight
Garnered by Thee within me, may no man
Unlock it but the loved one? Must I clasp
No child of my own womb if he be dead
Or come not back to me? O God, dear God,
I did not make myself: Thy strong desire
Consumes me. Help me! help me!' — On the night
I wrestled thus in prayer, divine content
Descended tranquilly and overbrimmed

My famished heart; the lurking dragon whirled
His jewelled mail away, his blood-stained fangs;
And at my chamber- window watching me.
And beckoning, and waiting to be born.
The seraph faces of my children pressed.
In widow's weeds I tarried one year more.
Then chose Sir Hilary from out my throng
Of honourable blandishers to be
The father of my children — stately then
And tall, a personable gentleman
Some ten years older than myself: sedate
He seemed and wise — his fame without a flaw,
I told him though I had no love to give
I should be proud to be his faithful wife
And bosom-friend. That pleased him best, he said —
Lying, because he strove to make of me
An instrument of pleasure for himself;
But like Zenobia, noblest of her sex,
I kept my babes unsullied. Look at them!"

She stepped behind her children, seven in all—
Four lustrous youths, three maidens lovelier
Than seraphs hallowed visionaries see.
"These are my witnesses." Emanuel
Bent towards them, blessing them. Sir Hilary,
Hell glimmering in his visage, gnawed his tongue,
And let his beaver down.

"My Bertha here"—
Taking her eldest daughter by the hand —
"Sleepless all night, this morning to my room
Came blushing with the dawn. Beside me couched.
She told the tale of passion Sigismund
Beneath the evening star had told to her.
And in my arms fell peacefully asleep."

At once a page attendant on the King
Vaulted the barrier, and took his post
Beside the younger Bertha, overjoyed
To find his suit accepted, and of right
Claiming a share in what should now befall
His lady's house. The elder Bertha smiled
A welcome, tender of any happiness
Even in her misery; then made an end.

"My daughter's passion wakened from the grave
The memory of the wonder-working stir
And daybreak of my womanhood. I stole

The ring — to me it seemed indeed a theft,
A crime of sacrilege against the past,
Which yet I had no courage to forgo —
From out the casket where I buried it
Upon my marriage-morn. Helpless I thrust
The pale thing in my breast, and took it forth,
And kissed it . . . out among the trees I ran.
The meadow-hay new-reaped ... I saw him come;
He kissed me after thirty years ... I God ..."
The younger Bertha caught her in her arms,
And dried her tears.

Well-pleased the King arose
To vindicate her fame; but Hilary cried,
"This was appealed to God, and He has judged:
There one adulterer lies; the other waits
The sentence of the King. Who looks with lust
Commits adultery. Be strong; do right.
Dare you annul God's manifest decree?

Do you believe in God, Emanuel —
No shifting thought of man's, a God?"
A poignant voice from out his hollow casque;
Whereat the King delayed the judgement dulled
By nerveless doubt.

But Bertha laughed, "Believe
In God!" — shaking her loosened mane of gold
From off her face, and with her heavy-lashed
And azure-watered eyelids clearing up
Her clouded vision — "I believe in God!
And He inspires me now to understand
His purpose in my lover's overthrow,

Doubtless He needed him in Heaven to be
His champion against some challenger,
Or to explore a new-made tract of worlds.
Me He requires to signify to men
That those obey Him best and do His will
Implicitly, who on themselves alone
Rely in peril of a tarnished name;
For power divine in plenitude enough
To conquer every ill endows us all,
If valiantly we give it scope to work
By taking on ourselves the total war.
Had Godfrey beaten Hilary, 'Oh ay' —
The gossips and the sponsors of report
Would certainly have made the accepted word —

'The hardy, brilliant lover overthrows
The age-bent husband.' Now myself can dear
From every foul aspersion Godfrey's fame,
Mine, and my children's. Wherefore I demand
The Ordeal by Fire, Emanuel."

"I grant it," said the King, feeling himself
Heroic: "I believe in God and you.
Choose, then: the bar; the ring?"

But Hilary said,
"The way of ploughshares heated hot remains
The ordeal provided by the law."

"The ploughshares!" said the King, held in the trap
Of code that men will set to catch themselves.
"None ever traverse them uncharred, and few
Escape with life."

But I uncharred shall pass,"
The victim said. "Sir, I appeal to God
Within me and about me and above
To bear me scathless through the fiercest test.
Heat hot your ploughshares — now!

Her children quailed
"No, mother — no!" they whispered.
What!" she cried,
"You also doubt your mother's chastity
And God's omnipotence and rectitude!"
Abashed they fell behind her.

Still the King
Debated with himself: but from the crowd
A tigrish clamour burst, and watering mouths
Gnashed as they roared, "The ploughshares! Heat them hot!"

"Hark!" said the King, "it is the voice of God!
Prepare the ordeal chosen and ordained."

So when the evening threw across the west
Fabrics of vapour fine as treasured lace —
Dishevelled, faded, stained with crimson, trailed
And dipped in sacramental chalices
Of sunset unforgotten while love lasts —
Upon the damasked meadow fires were built
Beside the sounding threshold of the sea:
Nine furnaces, fierce-tempered, wherewithal

The snoring bellows, plied by eager hands,
Imparted to the iron the sexual hate
Obscurely rankling in the heart of life,
And now unloosed against the innocent.
As at a fair men laughed obscenely, trolled
The vapid catches ballad-mongers hawked,
And munched the wares of wayside merchantmen.
Upon the City wall strange women climbed —
No nearer might they stand: men ruled it so —
To watch their sister's martyrdom, unawed,
Or with a dull disquietude, or to pray:
For even soulless women sometimes pray
As headless insects buzz. Emanuel
Sat in a chair of state, and gripped the arms,
Teeth clenched, eyes fixed, extorting from his soul
Belief that God would do what he desired.
Sir Hilary stood by, the ripened grudge
Of twenty years triumphant in his eyes,
And in his rigid heart a holy sense
Of dreadful duty done — one drop of gall.
One only in his vengeful cup: the King
In every charitable name had driven
The children, guarded, out of sight and sound
Of Bertha's hazard: thus the simpletons,
Who liked their father little and adored
The adulteress, were not to see the end!
Blindfolded, in her shroud, with naked feet.
She waited for the signal to advance.

"Is all prepared?" the King demanded. Ay;
All was prepared. Aghast and tremulous.
He turned to Bertha: "Are you ready, now?"

"Ready," she said, clear-voiced, "God helping me!"
"What is your plea?" he asked; for this the law required.

She answered: "If in thought or deed
I once betrayed my husband's trust, may death
Lay hold of me and drag me shrieking down
A branded corpse among the smouldering blades."

"In God's great heart the issue lies. Proceed."
This said, the King bent down his twitching face
In prayer; for even men of parts will pray
Against the wrong instead of smiting it,
Besotted with a creed.

The farriers,

Aglow, begrimed and moist with smoky sweat,
Their ready pinchers on the coulters clasped
And plucked them forth, sprinkling the dewy green
With jets of dying embers. Placed apart
At intervals irregular, the nine
Deep notes of carmine pulsed in unison
Upon the hissing turf. Trumpet and drum
Announced the ordeal; then softly raised
A Funeral dirge as Bertha, breathing quick,
Set out upon her march. She placed her foot,
Her naked buoyant foot, dew-drenched and white,
She placed it firmly on the first red edge,
Leapt half her height, and with a hideous cry
Fell down face-foremost brained upon the next.
They took her from among the smouldering blades,
A branded corpse, and laid her on the bier
Prepared: alive or dead, the record told
Of none who trod this fiery path uncharred.

The miserable King arose and turned
In haggard silence toward the city.

"Sir,"
Said Hilary in an icy voice, "the law
Exacts your sentence."

"Bloody, hellish beast!"
Burst out Emanuel, weak and broken,

"Sir,"
Said Hilary, "you stand for God, and must
Pronounce the doom which he has dumbly wrought.
You know the form."

Then sullenly the King:
"Bertha, the wife of Hilary, is proved
A foul adulteress upon her own appeal
To Heaven, and in the market-place forthwith
Shall be consumed by fire."

"So let it be,"
The multitude replied. So was it done.
And while the harlots and the prodigals
Jested and danced about the blazing corpse.
The moon, dispensing delegated light,
Behind the City stealthily arose;
And, fresh with scent of meadow-hay new reaped,
The land-breeze bore to many a mariner,

Outward or homeward bound, the sweetest news
Across the sounding threshold of the sea.

A BALLAD OF A COWARD

The trumpets pealed; the echoes sang
A tossing fugue; before it died,
Again the rending trumpets rang,
Again the phantom notes replied.

In galleries, on straining roofs.
At once ten thousand tongues were hushed.
When down the lists a storm of hoofs
From either border thundering rushed.

A knight whose arms were chased and set
With gold and gems, in fear withdrew
Before the fronts of tourney met,
Before the spears in splinters flew.

He reached the wilds. He cast away
His lance and shield and arms of price;
He turned his charger loose, and lay
Face-downwards in his cowardice.

His wife had seen the recreant fly:
She followed, found, and called his name
"Sweetheart, I will not have you die:
My love," she said, "can heal your shame."

Not long his vanity withstood
Her gentleness. He left his soul
To her; and her solicitude.
He being a coward, made him whole.

Yet was he blessed in heart and head;
Forgiving; of his riches free;
Wise was he too, and deeply read,
And ruled his earldom righteously.

A war broke out. With fateful speed
The foe, eluding watch and ward,
Conquered; and none was left to lead
The land, save this faint-hearted lord,

"Here is no shallow tournament,

No soulless, artificial fight.
Courageously, in deep content,
I go to combat for the right."

The hosts encountered: trumpets spoke;
Drums called aloud; the air was torn
With cannon, light by stifling smoke
Estopped, and shrieking battle born.

But he? — he was not in the van!
The vision of his child and wife?
Even that deserted him. He ran —
The coward ran to save his life.

The lowliest men would sooner face
A thousand dreadful deaths, than come
Before their loved ones in disgrace;
Yet this sad coward hurried home:

For, as he fled, his cunning heart
Declared he might be happy yet
In some retreat where Love and Art
Should swathe his soul against regret.

"My wife! my son! For their dear sakes,
He thought, "I save myself by flight."—
He reached his place. '* What comet shakes
Its baleful tresses on the night

Above my towers?" Alas, the foe
Had been before with sword and fire!
His loved ones in their blood lay low:
Their dwelling was their funeral pyre.

Then he betook him to a hill
Which in his happy times had been
His silent friend, meaning to kill
Himself upon its bosom green.

But an old mood at every tread
Returned; and with assured device
The wretched coward's cunning head
Distilled it into cowardice.

"A snowy owl on silent wings
Sweeps by; and, ah! I know the tune
The wayward night-wind sweetly sings
And dreaming birds in coverts croon.

"The cocks their muffled catches crow;
The river ripples dark and bright;
I hear the pastured oxen low.
And the whole rumour of the night.

"The moon comes from the wind-swept hearth
Of heaven; the stars beside her soar;
The seas and harvests of the earth
About her shadowy footsteps pour.

"But though remembrances, all wet
With happy tears, their tendrils coil
Close round my heart; though I be set
And rooted in the ruddy soil.

"My pulses with the planets leap;
The veil is rent before my face;
My aching nerves are mortised deep
In furthest cavities of space;

"Through the pervading ether speed
My thoughts that now the stars rehearse;
And should I take my life, the deed
Would disarray the universe."

Gross cowardice! Hope, while we breathe,
Can make the meanest prize his breath,
And still with starry garlands wreathe
The nakedness of life and death.

He wandered vaguely for a while;
Then thought at last to hide his sham
And self-contempt far in an isle
Among the outer deeps; but came,

Even there, upon a seaboard dim,
Where like the slowly ebbing tide
That weltered on the ocean's rim
With sanguine hues of sunset dyed,

The war still lingered. Suddenly,
Ere he could run, the bloody foam
Of battle burst about him; he.
Scarce knowing what he did, str home.

As those he helped began to fly,
Bidding him follow. "Nay," he said

"Nay; I die fighting — even I!"
And happy and amazed fell dead.

COMING

In every noble name
What are we waiting for?
We pray, and we declaim!
Are we afraid of war?
Drummer, beat the drum!
Trumpets, blow!
Anguished voices bid us come!
At last we go!

Shall Europe cry "God speed!"
To some less famous land?
Nay; who shall take the lead.
If England holds her hand?
Proud? We should be proud!
Drummer, beat the drum!
Anguished voices call aloud,
England, come!"

Upon the blood-stained sod
A helpless people bow;
We still have stood for God,
And shall we falter now?
The sword is in our hand;
Our step is on the sea;
We are coming, sister land.
To set you free!

BATTLE

The war of words is done;
The red-lipped cannon speak;
The battle has begun.

The web your speeches spun
Tears and blood shall streak;
The war of words is done.

Smoke enshrouds the sun;
Earth staggers at the shriek

Of battle new begun.

Poltroons and braggarts run:
Woe to the poor, the meek!
The war of words is done.

"And hope not now to shun
The doom that dogs the weak,"
Thunders every gun;

"Victory must be won."
When the red-lipped cannon speak.
The war of words is done,
The slaughter has begun.

THE HYMN OF ABDUL HAMID

Whene'er Thy mosque I trod
I heard my sabre sigh,
"There is no God but God;
Believe in Him or die!

"Abdul the Bless'd! You must
Pursue the Prophet's path!
Up! slake the eager lust
Of God's avenging wrath!"

Islam! a dreadful call!
Long, long I made delay.
"My back is at the wall:
Look, Lord; I stand at bay!

"The eagles throng," I cried,
"Expecting me to die:
The Powers my throne deride;
I am the Sick Man, I!"

But there my troops were ranked,
A weapon to my hand;
And still my sabre clanked,
"Go forth and purge the land!

At last Mohammed's sword.
The Key of Heaven and Hell,
I drew; and at my word
A hundred thousand fell,

God-hated: in their day.
Foul cumberers of the earth;
Now theirs is ours; and they.
Fuel for Shetan's hearth.

Though journalists proclaimed
That things were at the worst;
Though Ministers were blamed;
Though poets sang and cursed;

Though priests in every church
Prayed God to shield the right,
God left them in the lurch:
They were afraid to fight!

Words, words they slung; while we.
Indifferent to the cost.
Fulfilled God's high decree
In slaughtering the lost.

The Powers blasphemed beneath;
Above Heaven smiled delight;
Ho! Europe gnashed her teeth;
And Greece began to bite.

They fell into the pit
They dug for our dismay;
The biter soon was bit;
The spoilers are our prey!

The Sick Man? No; the Strong!
Prestige is ours again!
God gives us a new song
Like sunshine after rain.

Grasping a shadow, lo,
The Dog has lost his bone —
The Christian Dog! Even so!
Allah is God alone!

WAR-SONG

In anguish we uplift
A new unhallowed song:
The race is to the swift;

The battle to the strong.

Of old it was ordained
That we, in packs like curs,
Some thirty million trained
And licensed murderers,

In crime should live and act.
If cunning folk say sooth
Who flay the naked fact
And carve the heart of truth.

The rulers cry aloud,
"We cannot cancel war,
The end and bloody shroud
Of wrongs the worst abhor,

And order's swaddling band:
Know that relentless strife
Remains by sea and land
The holiest law of life.
From fear in every guise,
From sloth, from lust of pelf,
By war's great sacrifice
The world redeems itself.
War is the source, the theme
Of art; the goal, the bent
And brilliant academe
Of noble sentiment;
The augury, the dawn
Of golden times of grace;
The true catholicon,
And blood-bath of the race."

We thirty million trained
And licensed murderers,
Like zanies rigged, and chained
By drill and scourge and curse
In shackles of despair
We know not how to break —
What do we victims care
For art, what interest take
In things unseen, unheard?
Some diplomat no doubt
Will launch a heedless word.
And lurking war leap out!

We spell-bound armies then.

Huge brutes in dumb distress,
Machines compact of men
Who once had consciences.
Must trample harvests down —
Vineyard, and corn and oil;
Dismantle town by town,
Hamlet and homestead spoil
On each appointed path.
Till lust of havoc light
A blood-red blaze of wrath
In every frenzied sight.

In many a mountain-pass.
Or meadow green and fresh,
Mass shall encounter mass
Of shuddering human flesh;
Opposing ordnance roar
Across the swaths of slain.
And blood in torrents pour
In vain — always in vain,
For war breeds war again!

The shameful dream is past,
The subtle maze untrod:
We recognize at last
That war is not of God.
Wherefore we now uplift
Our new unhallowed song:
The race is to the swift.
The battle to the strong.

THE BADGE OF MEN

"In shuttered rooms let others grieve,
And coffin thought in speech of lead;
I'll tie my heart upon my sleeve:
It is the Badge of Men," he said.

His friends forsook him: "Who was he!"
Even beggars passed him with a grin:
Physicians called it lunacy;
And priests, the unpardonable sin.

He strove, he struck for standing-ground:
They beat him humbled from the field;
For though his sword was keen, he found

His mangled heart a feeble shield.

He slunk away, and sadly sought
The wilderness — false friend of woe,
"Man is The Enemy," he thought;
But Nature proved a fiercer foe:

The vampire sucked, the vulture tore,
And the old dragon left its den,
Agape to taste the thing he wore —
The ragged, bleeding Badge of Men.

"Against the Fates there steads no charm,
For every force takes its own part:
I'll wear a buckler on my arm,
And in my bosom hide my heart!"

But in his bosom prisoned fast
It pained him more than when it beat
Upon his sleeve; and so he cast
His trouble to the ghouls to eat.

Back to the city, there and then
He ran; and saw, through all disguise,
On every sleeve the Badge of Men:
For truth appears to cruel eyes.

Straight with his sword he laid about,
And hacked and pierced their hearts, until
The beaten terror-stricken rout
Begged on their knees to know his will.

He said, "I neither love nor hate;
I would command in everything."
They answered him, "Heartless and great!
Your slaves we are: be you our king!"

THE UNRESIGNED MOURNER

Unwilling tears on silken lashes,
Sighs and lamentations deep!
Why do you sit in dust and ashes,
Lady, lady, why do you weep?

"Because, although my soul that hastened
To welcome love Is now bereft

Of happiness, I live unchastened,
And curse the bitter anguish left."

THE GIFT

Solacing tears,
The suppliant's sigh,
Repentant years
The fates deny;
But tortured breath
Has one ally,
The gift of death.
The power to die.

EARTH TO EARTH

Where the region grows without a lord,
Between the thickets emerald-stoled,
In the woodland bottom the virgin sward,
The cream of the earth, through depths of mold
O'erflowing wells from secret cells.
While the moon and the sun keep watch and ward,
And the ancient world is never old.

Here, alone, by the grass-green hearth
Tarry a little: the mood will come!
Feel your body a part of earth;
Rest and quicken your thought at home;
Take your ease with the brooding trees;
Join in their deep-down silent mirth
The crumbling rock and the fertile loam.

Listen and watch! The wind will sing;
And the day go out by the western gate;
The night come up on her darkling wing;
And the stars with flaming torches wait.
Listen and see! And love and be
The day and the night and the world-wide thing
Of strength and hope you contemplate.

No lofty Patron of Nature! No;
Nor a callous devotee of Art!
But the friend and the mate of the high and the low,
And the pal to take the vermin's part,

Your inmost thought divinely wrought,
In the grey earth of your brain aglow
With the red earth burning in your heart.

MY LILY

I must sing you a song.
Or my heart will break.
For all the night long
I lie awake,
And all the day through
I am sorry like you
For nobody's sake,
For nobody's sake.
My lily, my lily
You and I,
My lily, sad lily!

Since the day has the sun.
And the night the moon,
Though love we have none,
How soon, how soon
Our hearts may awake
For somebody's sake,
And our lives be in tune,
Our lives be in tune,
My lily, my lily
You and I,
My lily, sweet lily!

PRINCE OF THE FAIRIES

Over the mountains, happy and bold,
The Prince of the Fairies a-wooing came
With a ring and a brooch and a crown of gold,
And a heart of the same, a heart of the same!
And each of them, all of them, every one
He would lay at her feet
If he only could meet
The loveliest maiden under the sun.

They hated him heartily, burghers and peers;
For the merchants' daughters were ready to die
And the queens of the earth would have given their ears

For a touch of his hand or a glance of his eye:
But he laughed and he said to them every one,
"Now, by yea and by nay,
I have nothing to say
Except to the loveliest under the sun."

Back o'er the mountains, hardly so bold,
The Prince of the Fairies lamenting came,
Till he met in the way with her curls of gold
And her heart of the same, her heart of the same,
A damsel a- watching her geese every one:
"Lo," he shouted, "my queen!
For at last I have seen
The loveliest maiden under the sun!"

THE STOOP OF RHENISH

When dogs in office frown you down,
And malice smirches your renown;
When fools and knaves your blunders twit,
And melancholy dries your wit;
Be no more dull
But polish and plenish
Your empty skull
With a stoop of Rhenish.
Drink by the card.
Drink by the score,
Drink by the yard.
Drink evermore.

When seamy sides begin to show,
And dimples into wrinkles grow;
When care comes in by hook or crook
And settles at your ingle-nook,
Never disdain
To polish and plenish
Your rusty brain
With a stoop of Rhenish.
Drink by the card,
Drink by the score.
Drink by the yard,
Drink evermore!

When hope gets up before the dawn,
And every goose appears a swan;
When time and tide, and chance and fate

Like lackeys on your wishes wait;
Then fill the bowl.
And polish and plenish
Your happy soul
With a stoop of Rhenish,
Drink by the card,
Drink by the score.
Drink by the yard.
Drink evermore!

MATINEES

I

Night went down; the twilight ceased;
The moon withdrew her phantom flame;
In pearl and silver out of the east,
Pallid and vigilant, morning came:
By heath and hill with trumpets shrill
The orient wind declared his name: —

"Morning! Morning! Mighty, alone,
Light, the light, whose titles are
Courage and hope, ascends his throne
Over the head of every star:
Terror and pain are chained and slain,
And mournful shadows flee afar."

II

From the night-haunt where vapours crowd
The airy outskirts of the earth
A winding caravan of cloud
Rose when the morning's punctual heart!
Began to charm the winds and skies
With odours fresh and golden dyes.

It made a conquest of the sun.
And tied his beams; but, in the game
Of hoodman-blind, the rack, outdone.
Beheld the brilliant captive claim
Forfeit on forfeit, as he pressed
The mountains to his burning breast.

Above the path by vapours trod

A ringing causey seemed to be,
Whereby the orient, silver-shod.
Rode out across the Atlantic sea.
An embassy of valour sent
Under the echoing firmament.

And while the hearkener divined
A clanging cavalcade on high.
This rush and trample of the wind
Arose among the tree-tops nigh.
For mystery is the craft profound.
The sign, and ancient trade of sound.

An unseen roadman breaking flint.
If echo and the winds conspire
To dedicate his morning's stint,
May beat a tune out, dew and fire
So wrought that heaven might lend an ear,
And Ariel hush his harp to hear.

HOLIDAY AT HAMPTON COURT

Scales of pearly cloud inlay
North and south the turquoise sky.
While the diamond lamp of day
Quenchless burns, and time on high
A moment halts upon his way
Bidding noon again good-bye.

Gaffers, gammers, huzzies, louts,
Couples, gangs, and families
Sprawling, shake, with Babel-shouts
Bluff King Hal's funereal trees;
And eddying groups of stare-abouts
Quiz the sandstone Hercules.

When their tongues and tempers tire,
Harry and his little lot
Condescendingly admire
Lozenge-bed and crescent-plot.
Aglow with links of azure fire.
Pansy and forget-me-not.

Where the emerald shadows rest
In the lofty woodland aisle,
Chaffing lovers quaintly dressed

Chase and double many a mile.
Indifferent exiles in the west
Making love in cockney style.

Now the echoing palace fills;
Men and women, girls and boys
Trample past the swords and frills,
Kings and Queens and trulls and toys;
Or listening loll on window-sills,
Happy amateurs of noise!

That for pictured rooms of state!
Out they hurry, wench and knave.
Where beyond the palace-gate
Dusty legions swarm and rave.
With laughter, shriek, inane debate,
Kentish fire and comic stave.

Voices from the river call;
Organs hammer tune on tune;
Larks triumphant over all
Herald twilight coming soon.
For as the sun begins to fall
Near the zenith gleams the moon.

IN THE ISLE OF DOGS

While the water-wagon's ringing showers
Sweetened the dust with a woodland smell,
"Past noon, past noon, two sultry hours,"
Drowsily fell
From the schoolhouse clock
The Isle of Dogs by Millwall Dock.

Mirrored in shadowy windows draped
With ragged net or half-drawn blind
Bowesprits, masts, exactly shaped
To woo or fight the wind,
Like monitors of guilt
By Strength and beauty sent,
Disgraced the shameful houses built
To furnish rent.

From the pavements and the roofs
In shimmering volumes wound
The wrinkled heat;

Distant hammers, wheels and hoofs,
A turbulent pulse of sound,
Southward obscurely beat,
The only utterance of the afternoon.
Till on a sudden in the silent street
An organ-man drew up and ground
The Old Hundredth tune.

Forthwith the pillar of cloud that hides the past
Burst into flame.
Whose alchemy transmuted house and mast,
Street, dockyard, pier and pile:
By magic sound the Isle of Dogs became
A northern isle —
A green isle like a beryl set
In a wine-coloured sea,
Shadowed by mountains where a river met
The ocean's arm extended royally.

There also in the evening on the shore
An old man ground the Old Hundredth tune,
An old enchanter steeped in human lore,
Sad-eyed, with whitening beard, and visage lank:
Not since and not before,
Under the sunset or the mellowing moon.
Has any hand of man's conveyed
Such meaning in the turning of a crank.

Sometimes he played
As if his box had been
An organ in an abbey richly lit;
For when the dark invaded day's demesne,
And the sun set in crimson and in gold;
When idlers swarmed upon the esplanade,
And a late steamer wheeling towards the quay
Struck founts of silver from the darkling sea,
The solemn tune arose and shook and rolled
Above the throng,
Above the hum and tramp and bravely knit
All hearts in common memories of song.

Sometimes he played at speed;
Then the Old Hundredth like a devil's mass
Instinct with evil thought and evil deed,
Rang out in anguish and remorse. Alas!
That men must know both Heaven and
Hell!
Sometimes the melody

Sang with the murmuring surge;
And with the winds would tell
Of peaceful graves and of the passing bell.
Sometimes it pealed across the bay
A high triumphal dirge,
A dirge

For the departing undefeated day.
A noble tune, a high becoming mate
Of the capped mountains and the deep broad firth;
A simple tune and great.
The fittest utterance of the voice of earth.

AFTERNOON

The hostess of the sky, the moon,
Already stoops to entertain
The golden light of afternoon.
And the wan earthshine from the plain.

No rustling wings, no voices warp
The ripened stillness of the day;
Behind the Downs the sheltered thorpe
Expectant overhangs the way.

What laughter, whisper, sigh or groan,
A hazardous, a destined sound,
Shall first usurp the airy throne
Where silence rules with twilight crowned?

Hark! hark! an antique noise! Across
The road the bellows fires anew
With jar and sough the hissing dross.
Close-raked about the half-wrought shoe.

From the swart chimney lilac smoke,
The blacksmith's prayer, to heaven ascends;
The hammers double stroke on stroke;
The stubborn iron sparkling bends.

Then voices near and far break out;
The starlings in the tree-tops scold;
The larks against each other shout;
The blackbirds scatter pearl and gold;

The jackdaws prate; the cuckoos call;

And shrill enough to reach the spheres
Resounds the brazen madrigal
Of half a hundred chanticleers.

INSOMNIA

He wakened quivering on a golden rack
Inlaid with gems: no sign of change, no fear
Or hope of death came near;
Only the empty ether hovered black
About him stretched upon his living bier,
Of old by Marlin's Master deftly wrought:
Two Seraphim of Gabriel's helpful race
In that far nook of space
With iron levers wrenched and held him taut.

The Seraph at his head was Agony;
Delight, more terrible, stood at his feet:
Their sixfold pinions beat
The darkness, or were spread immovably,
Poising the rack, whose jewelled fabric meet
To strain a god, did fitfully unmask
With olive light of chrysoprases dim
The smiling Seraphim
Implacably intent upon their task.

THE LAST ROSE

"Oh, which is the last rose?"
A blossom of no name.
At midnight the snow came;
At daybreak a vast rose.
In darkness unfurled,
O'er-petaled the world.
Its odourless pallor
Blossomed forlorn,
Till radiant valour
Established the morn —
Till the night
Was undone
In her fight
With the sun.

The brave orb in state rose

And crimson he shone first;
While from the high vine
Of heaven the dawn burst.
Staining the great rose
From sky-line to sky-line.

The red rose of morn
A white rose at noon turned;
But at sunset reborn,
All red again soon burned.
Then the pale rose of noonday
Re-bloomed in the night,
And spectrally white
In the light
Of the moon lay.

But the vast rose
Was scentless,
And this is the reason:
When the blast rose
Relentless,
And brought in due season
The snow-rose, the last rose
Congealed in its breath,
There came with it treason;
The traitor was Death.

In lee-valleys crowded,
The sheep and the birds
Were frozen and shrouded
In flights and in herds.
In highways
And byways
The young and the old
Were tortured and maddened
And killed by the cold.
But many were gladdened
By the beautiful last rose.
The blossom of no name
That came when the snow came.
In darkness unfurled —
The wonderful vast rose
That filled all the world.

The flowers with dust disgraced
Droop in garth and plain;
But the summer tempests haste
With lustral rain.

The banded vapour rolls,
Shadowing hill and town;
Anon the thunder tolls,
The showers come down.

Margents where the salt winds pass»
The freshened sea-pinks fret;
The roses change to hippocras
The heaven's pearly sweat;

And the flowers all shine and all the grass
Like jewels newly set,
Sapphire bright and chrysolite,
And emeralds dripping wet.

Like smoke from a happy hearth,
Out of the meads and the bowers,
The spicy dust of the moistened earth
And the rainy scent of the flowers
Translate to silence sweet the mirth
Of the silvery ringing showers.

THE PRICE

Terrible is the price
Of beginning anew, of birth;
For Death has loaded dice.

Men hurry and hide like mice;
But they cannot evade the Earth,
And Life, Death's fancy price.

A blossom once or twice.
Love lights on Summer's hearth;
But Winter loads the dice.

In jangling shackles of ice,
Ragged and bleeding. Mirth
Pays the Piper's price.

The dance is done in a trice:

Death belts his bony girth;
And struts, and rattles his dice.

Let Virtue play or Vice,
Beside his sombre firth
Life is the lowest price
Death wins with loaded dice.

THE UNKNOWN

To brave and to know the unknown
Is the high world's motive and mark.
Though the way with snares be strewn.

The Earth itself alone
Wheels through the light and the dark
Onward to meet the unknown.

Each soul, upright or prone,
While the owl sings or the lark,
Must pass where the bones are strewn.

Power on the loftiest throne
Can fashion no certain ark
That shall stem and outride the unknown.

Beauty must doff her zone,
Strength trudge unarmed and stark.
Though the way with eyes be strewn.

This only can atone,
The high world's motive and mark,
To brave and to know the unknown
Though the way with fire be strewn.

WAITING

Within unfriendly walls
We starve — or starve by stealth.
Oxen fatten in their stalls;
You guard the harrier's health:
They never can be criminals.
And can't compete for wealth.
From the mansion and the palace

Is there any help or hail
For the tenants of the alleys,
Of the workhouse and the jail?

Though lands await our toil.
And earth half-empty rolls,
Cumberers of English soil.
We cringe for orts and doles —
Prosperity's accustomed foil,
Millions of useless souls.
In the gutters and the ditches
Human vermin festering lurk —
We, the rust upon your riches;
We, the flaw in all your work.

Come down from where you sit;
We look to you for aid.
Take us from the miry pit,
And lead us undismayed:
Say, "Even you, outcast, unfit.
Forward with sword and spade!"
And myriads of us idle
Would thank you through our tears,
Though you drove us with a bridle,
And a whip about our ears!

From cloudy cape to cape
The teeming waters seethe;
Golden grain and purple grape
The regions overwreathe.
Will no one help us to escape?
We scarce have room to breathe.
You might try to understand us:
We are waiting night and day
For a captain to command us.
And the word we must obey.

THE ARISTOCRAT

They sundered usage like a wedge;
They swept the ancients from their stools;
By piracy, by sacrilege,
By war, across the necks of fools
A royal road, the strong men strode.
But other times have other tools.

The warlord and the churchlord stir
The pulses of the world no more;
The trader and the usurer
Have passed the lion-guarded door;
The praise, the prayer, the incensed air
Ascend to us from every share.

A Money-lord, unheralded,
I issue from a vulgar strain
Of churls, who spiced their daily bread
With hungry toil in sun and rain,
A secret dower of patience power
And courage in my blood and brain.

Though Corner, Trust and Company
Are subtler than the old-time tools.
The Sword, the Rack, the Gallowstree,
I traverse none of Nature's rules;
I lay my yoke on feeble folk.
And march across the necks of fools.

My friends and foes adventured much;
But elbowing iron pots the delf
Go down in shards; or some rude touch
Of fact installs upon the shelf
Souls slimly cast: for me, I last,
I wiser, braver, more myself.

THE OUTCAST

Soul, be your own
Pleasance and mart,
A land unknown,
A state apart.

Scowl, and be rude
Should love entice;
Call gratitude
The costliest vice.

Deride the ill
By fortune sent;
Be scornful still
If foes repent.

When curse and stone

Are hissed and hurled.
Aloof, alone
Disdain the world.

Soul, disregard
The bad, the good;
Be haughty, hard,
Misunderstood.

Be neutral; spare
No humblest lie,
And overbear
Authority.

Laugh wisdom down;
Abandon fate;
Shame the renown
Of all the great.

Dethrone the past;
Deed, vision — naught
Avails at last
Save your own thought

Though on all hands
The powers unsheathe
Their lightning-brands
And from beneath.

And from above
One curse be hurled
With scorn, with love
Affront the world.

THE PIONEER

Why, he never can tell;
But, without a doubt.
He knows very well
He must trample out
Through forest and fell
The world about
A way for himself,
A way for himself.

By sun and star.

Forlorn and lank.
O'er cliff and scar,
O'er bog and bank.
He hears afar
The expresses clank,
"You'll never get there.
You'll never get there!"

His bones and bread
Poor Turlygod
From his wallet spread
On the grass-green sod.
And stared and said
With a mow and a nod,
"Whither away, sir.
Whither away?"

"I'm going alone.
Though Hell forfend.
By a way of my own
To the bitter end."
He gnawed a bone
And snarled, "My friend,
You'll soon get there,
You'll soon get there."

But whether or no.
The world is round;
And he still must go
Through depths profound,
O'er heights of snow,
On virgin ground
To find a grave.
To find a grave.

For he knows very well
He must trample out
Through Heaven and Hell,
With never a doubt,
A way of his own
The world about.

THE HERO

My thought sublimes
A common deed;

In evil times
In utmost need,
My spirit climbs
Where dragons breed.

Nor will I trip
Even at the hiss
On the drawn lip
Of the abyss:
My footsteps grip
The precipice.

Applause and blame
Let prophets share:
My secret aim
The deed I dare,
My own acclaim
Comprise my care.

Above the laws,
Against the light
That overawes
The world I fight
And win, because
I have the might.

ECLOGUES

I

The Merchantman, The Markethaunters

The Markethaunters
Now, while our money is piping hot
From the mint of our toil that coins the sheaves,
Merchantman, merchantman, what have you got
In your tabernacle hung with leaves?
What have you got?
The sun rides high;
Our money is hot;
We must buy, buy, buy!

The Merchantman
I come from the elfin king's demesne
With chrysolite, hyacinth, tourmaline;
I have emeralds here of living green;

I have rubies, each like a cup of wine;
And diamonds, diamonds that never have been
Outshone by eyes the most divine I

The Markethaunters

Jewellery? — Baubles; bad for the soul;
Desire of the heart and lust of the eye!
Diamonds, indeed! We wanted coal.
What else do you sell? Come, sound your cry!
Our money is hot;
The night draws nigh;
What have you got
That we want to buy?

The Merchantman

I have here enshrined the soul of the rose
Exhaled in the land of the daystar's birth;
I have casks whose golden staves enclose
Eternal youth, eternal mirth;
And cordials that bring repose,
And the tranquil night, and the end of the earth.

The Markethaunters

Rapture of wine? But it never pays:
We must keep our common-sense alert.
Raisins are healthier, medicine says —
Raisins and almonds for dessert.
But we want to buy;
For our money is hot.
And age draws nigh:
What else have you got?

The Merchantman

I have lamps that gild the lustre of noon;
Shadowy arrows that pierce the brain;
Dulcimers strung with beams of the moon;
Psalteries fashioned of pleasure and pain;
A song and a sword and a haunting tune
That may never be offered the world again.

The Market haunters

Dulcimers! psalteries! Whom do you mock?
Arrows and songs? We have axes to grind!
Shut up your booth and your mouldering stock,
For we never shall deal. — Come away; let us find
What the others have got
We must buy, buy, buy;
For our money is hot.

And death draws nigh,

II

The Fool, Worldly Wiseman

The Fool
In haste, ere my senses wither,
I travel and search the night:
Whence am I? what am I? whither?
I must have fullest light.

Worldly Wiseman
That is your cry! Take heed;
Look to your steps, I say.
Return, for now, indeed,
Soul-traps beset your way:
Some man-devouring creed
Will seize you for a prey —
Some engine, baited bright
With immortality
Will drag you out of sight
And rend you: know that he
Who must have fullest light
Plots for his enemy.

In youth we hope; with age
The bargain seems unjust;
But yet though none engage
For Death's cold dust to dust —
The fixed, the only wage —
We take our doom on trust.

Such is the gentle rede
That prudent men embrace —
No fierce, enchanting creed
To live for in disgrace.
But good enough at need
In any market-place.
Stare at the darkness, shout
Your frenzied how and why.
No ghost will whet your doubt^
No echo give reply;
Only the world will flout,
And fortune pass you by.

The Fool
Let chance sway hither and thither,
And the world be wrong or right.
Here, now, ere my sinews wither,
I wrestle with infinite night:
Whence am I? what am I? whither?
I will have fullest light.

III

Artist, **Votary**

Votary
What gloomy outland region have I won?

Artist
This is the Vale of Hinnom. What are you?

Votary
A Votary of Life. I thought this tract,
With rubbish choked, had been a thorough-fare
For many a decade now.

Artist
No highway here!
And those who enter never can return.

Votary
But since my coming is an accident —

Artist
All who inhabit Hinnom enter there
By accident, carelessly cast aside,
Or self-inducted in an evil hour.

Votary
But I shall walk about it and go forth.

Artist
I said so when I came; but I am here.

Votary
What brought you hither?

Artist
Chance, no other power:
My tragedy is common to my kind. —

Once from a mountain-top at dawn I saw
My life pass by, a pageant of the age.
Enchanting many minds with sound and light,
Array and colour, deed, device and spell.
And to myself I said aloud, "When thought
And passion shall be rooted deep, and fleshed
In all experience man may dare, yet front
His own interrogation unabashed:
Winged also, and inspired to cleave with might
Abysses and the loftiest firmament:
When my capacity and art are ranked
Among the powers of nature, and the world
Awaits my message, I will paint a scene
Of life and death, so tender, so humane,
That lust and avarice lulled awhile, shall gaze
With open countenances; broken hearts,
The haunt, the shrine, and wailing-place of woe,
Be comforted with respite unforeseen,
And immortality reprieve despair."
The vision beckoned me; the prophecy,
That smokes and thunders in the blood of youth,
Compelled unending effort, treacherous
Decoys of doom although these tokens were.
Across the wisdom and the wasted love
Of some who barred the way my pageant stepped:
"Thus are all triumphs paved," I said; but soon,
Entangled in the tumult of the times,
Sundered and wrecked, it ceased to pace my thought,

Wherein alone its airy nature strode;
While the smooth world, whose lord I deemed myself,
Unsheathed its claws and blindly struck me down,
Mangled my soul for sport, and cast me out
Alive in Hinnom where human offal rots.
And fires are heaped against the tainted air.

Votary
Escape!

Artist
I tried, as you will try; and then,
Dauntless, I cried, "At midnight, darkly lit
By drifts of flame whose ruddy varnish dyes
The skulls and rounded knuckles light selects
Flickering upon the refuse of despair.
Here, as it should the costly pageant ends;
And here with my last strength, since I am I,
Here will I paint my scene of life and death:

Not that I dreamt of when the eager dawn.
And inexperience, stubborn parasite
Of youth and manhood, flattered in myself
And in a well-pleased following, vanities
Of hope, belief, good-will, the embroidered stuff
That masks the cruel eyes of destiny;
But a new scene profound and terrible
As Truth, the implacable antagonist.
And yet most tender, burning, bitter-sweet
As are the briny tears and crimson drops
Of human anguish, inconsolable
Throughout all time, and wept in every age
By open wounds and cureless, such as I,
Whence issues nakedly the heart of life."

Votary
What canvas and what colour could you find
To paint in Hinnom so intense a scene?

Artist
I found and laid no colour. Look about!
On the flame-roughened darkness whet your eyes.
This needs no deeper hue; this is the thing:
Millions of people huddled out of sight.
The offal of the world.

Votary
I see them now,
In groups, in multitudes, in hordes, and some
Companionless, ill-lit by tarnished fire
Under the towering darkness ceiled with smoke;
Erect, supine, kneeling or prone, but all
Sick-hearted and aghast among the bones.

Artist
Here pine the subtle souls that had no root,
No home below, until disease or shame
Undid the once-so-certain destiny
Imagined for the Brocken-sprite of self.
While earth, which seemed a pleasant inn of dreams,
Unveiled a tedious death-bed and a grave.

Votary
I see! The disillusioned geniuses
Who fain would make the world sit up, by Heaven!
And dig God in the ribs, and who refuse
Their own experience: would-bes, theorists.
Artistic natures, falled reformers, knaves

And fools incompetent or overbold.
Broken evangelists and debauchees.
Inebriates, criminals, cowards, virtual slaves.

Artist
The world is old; and countless strains of blood
Are now effete: these loathsome ruined lives
Are innocent — if life itself be good.
Inebriate, coward, artist, criminal —
The nicknames unintelligence expels
Remorse with when the conscience hints that all
Are guilty of the misery of one.
Look at these women: broken chalices,
Whose true aroma of the spring is spilt
In thankless streets and with the sewage blent.

Votary
Harlots, you mean; the scavengers of love.
Who sweep lust from our thresholds — needful brooms
In every age; the very bolts indeed
That clench and rivet solidarity.
All this is as it has been and shall be:
I see it, note it, and go hence. Farewell.

Artist
Here I await you.

Votary
There is no way out.

Artist
But we are many. What? So pinched and pale
At once! Weep, and take courage. This is best,
Because the alternative is not to be.

Votary
But I am nothing yet, have made no mark
Upon my time; and, worse than nothing now.
Must wither in a nauseous heap of tares.
Why am I outcast who so loved the world?
How did I reach this place? Hush! Let me think.
I said — what did I say and do? Nothing to mourn.
I trusted life, and life has led me here.

Artist
Where dull endurance only can avail.
Scarcely a tithe of men escape this fate;
And not a tithe of those who suffer know

Their utter misery.

Votary
And must this be
Now and for ever, and has it always been?

Artist
Worse now than ever and ever growing worse.
Men as they multiply use up mankind
In greater masses and in subtler ways:
Ever more opportunity, more power
For intellect, the proper minister
Of life, that will usurp authority.
With lightning at its beck and prisoned clouds.
I mean that electricity and steam
Have set a barbarous fence about the earth,
And made the oceans and the continents
Preserved estates of crafty gather-alls;
Have loaded labour with a shotted chain.
And raised the primal curse a thousand powers.

Votary
What! Are there honest labourers outcast here?
Dreamers, pococurantes, wanton bloods
In plenty and to spare; but surely work
Attains another goal than Hinnom!

Artist
Look!
Seared by the sun and carved by cold or blanched
In darkness; gnarled and twisted all awry
By rotting fogs; lamed, limb-lopped, cankered, burst,
The outworn workers!

Votary
I take courage then!
Since workers here abound it must be right
That men should end in Hinnom.

Artist
Right! How right?
The fable of the world till now records
Only the waste of life: the conquerors,
Tyrants and oligarchs, and men of ease,
Among the myriad nations, peoples, tribes.
Need not be thought of: earth's inhabitants,
Man, ape, dinornis for a moment breathe,
In misery die, and to oblivion

Are dedicated all. Consider still
The circumstance that most appeals to men:
Eternal siege and ravage of the source
Of being, of beauty, and of all delight.
The hell of whoredom. God! The hourly waste
Of women in the world since time began!

Votary
I think of it.

Artist
And of the waste of men
In war — pitiful soldiers, battle-harlots.

Votary
That also I consider.

Artist
Weaklings, fools
In millions who must end disastrously;
The willing hands and hearts, in millions too.
Paid with perdition for a life of toil;
The blood of women, a constant sacrifice,
Staining the streets and every altar-step;
The blood of men poured out in endless wars;
No hope, no help; the task, the stripes, the woe
Augmenting with the ages. Right, you say!

Votary
Do you remember how the moon appears
Illumining the night?

Artist
What has the moon
To do with Hinnom?

Votary
Call the moon to mind
Can you? Or have you quite forgotten all
The magic of her beams?

Artist
Oh no! The moon
Is the last memory of ample thought.
Of joy and loveliness that one forgets
In this abode. Since first the tide of life
Began to ebb and flow in human veins.
The targe of lovers' looks, their brimming fount

Of dreams and chalice of their sighs; with peace
And deathless legend clad and crowned, the moon!

Votary
But I adore it with a newer love,
Because it is the offal of the globe.
When from the central nebula our orb,
Outflung, set forth upon its way through space,
Still towards its origin compelled to lean
And grope in molten tides, a belt of fire,
Home-sick, burst off at last, and towards the sun
Whirling, far short of its ambition fell,
Insphered a little distance from the earth
There to bethink itself and wax and wane.
The moon!

Artist
I see! I know! You mean that you
And I, and foiled ambitions every one
In every age; the outworn labourers,
Pearls of the sewer, idlers, armies, scroyles,
The offal of the world, will somehow be —
Are now a lamp by night, although we deem
Ourselves disgraced, forlorn; even as the moon.
The scum and slag of earth, that, if it feels,
Feels only sterile pain, gladdens the mountains
And the spacious sea.

Votary
I mean it. And I mean
That the deep thoughts of immortality
And of our alienage, inventing gods
And paradise and wonders manifold.
Are rooted in the centre. We are fire,
Cut off and cooled a while; and shall return,
The earth and all thereon that live and die,
To be again candescent in the sun.
Or in the sun's intenser, purer source.
What matters Hinnom for an hour or two?
Arise and let us sing; and, singing, build
A tabernacle even with these ghastly bones.

John Davidson – A Short Biography

John Davidson was born at Barrhead, East Renfrewshire on 11th April 1857, the son of Alexander Davidson, an Evangelical Union minister and Helen née Crocket of Elgin.

In 1862 the family moved to Greenock and Davidson began his education at Highlanders' Academy. From there he began his career, aged a mere 13, at the chemical laboratory of Walker's Sugarhouse refinery. A year later he returned to Highlander's, this time as a pupil teacher.

During his later employment at the Public Analysts' Office, 1870–71 he developed a keen interest in science which later became an important characteristic of his poetry. He returned once again to the Highlander's Academy, this time for four years, in 1872, again as a pupil teacher. In 1876 he spent a year at Edinburgh University before his first scholastic employment at Alexander's Charity, Glasgow which led to short periods of employment at various other schools over the following half a dozen years.

This led to a stint at Morrison's Academy in Crieff (1885–88), and in a private school at Greenock (1888–89).

In 1885 Davidson married Margaret McArthur and the marriage produced two children, Alexander (born in 1887) and Menzies (born in 1889).

Davidson's first published work was 'Bruce, A Chronicle Play', written in the Elizabethan style, and published by a local Glasgow imprint in 1886. Four other plays quickly followed; 'Smith, A Tragic Farce' (1888), 'An Unhistorical Pastoral' (1889), 'A Romantic Farce' (1889), and then the somewhat brilliant pantomime 'Scaramouch in Naxos' (1889).

By now he was very much immersed in literature and, in 1889, he ventured to London where he frequented the famous Fleet Street pub 'Ye Olde Cheshire Cheese' and joined the 'Rhymers' Club', a poets group that was based there.

Davidson was a prolific and hard-working writer. As well as his plays he wrote for the Speaker, the Glasgow Herald, and several other papers. He also wrote and had published several novels and tales, with perhaps the best being 'Perfervid' (1890).

With his reputation gradually providing an income he was also able to explore his true medium; Verse. 'In a Music Hall and Other Poems' (1891) together with 'Fleet Street Eclogues' (1893) were ample proof that he possessed a quite rare, genuine and distinctive poetic gift. Praise came from his peers including George Gissing and WB Yeats who wrote that it was: 'An example of a new writer seeking out new subject matter, new emotions'.

Davidson now turned further and further towards verse. In 1894 he published his most popular volume, 'Ballads and Songs' (1894), and this was followed by a further 'Fleet Street Eclogues' (Second Series) (1896) and by 'New Ballads' (1897) and 'The Last Ballad' (1899).

Davidson was a prolific writer. Besides the works cited, he wrote many other works including, 'The Wonderful Mission of Earl Lavender' (1895), a novel which extends his literary canon to flagellation erotica. He also contributed an introduction to Shakespeare's Sonnets (Renaissance edition, 1908), which, like his various prefaces and essays, shows him to be a subtle literary critic.

As the new century dawned Davidson was hard at work on a series of 'Testaments', in which he gave definite expression to his philosophy and these were published over a seven year period; 'The

Testament of a Vivisector' (1901), 'The Testament of a Man Forbid' (1901), 'The Testament of an Empire Builder' (1902), and 'The Testament of John Davidson' (1908).

Though he played down any thought of himself as a philosopher, he expounded an original philosophy which was at once materialistic and aristocratic.

His later verse, which is often fine rhetoric rather than poetry, expressed his belief which is summed up in the last words that he wrote, "Men are the universe become conscious; the simplest man should consider himself too great to be called after any name." Davidson professed to reject all existing philosophies, including that of Nietzsche, as inadequate. The poet planned to expand and expound on his revolutionary creed in a trilogy entitled 'God and Mammon'. Only two plays, however, were written, 'The Triumph of Mammon' (1907) and 'Mammon and his Message' (1908).

In addition to his own work Davidson was a noted translator of other works which included Montesquieu's 'Lettres Persanes' (1892), François Coppée's 'Pour la Couronne' in 1896 and Victor Hugo's 'Ruy Blas' in 1904, the former being produced as, 'For the Crown', at the Lyceum Theatre in 1896, the latter as 'A Queen's Romance' at the Imperial Theatre.

Frank Harris, a member of the Rhymers' Club and himself a writer of erotic literature described him in 1889 as: "... a little below middle height, but strongly built with square shoulders and remarkably fine face and head; the features were almost classically regular, the eyes dark brown and large, the forehead high, the hair and moustache black. His manners were perfectly frank and natural; he met everyone in the same unaffected kindly human way; I never saw a trace in him of snobbishness or incivility. Possibly a great man, I said to myself, certainly a man of genius, for simplicity of manner alone is in England almost a proof of extraordinary endowment."

In 1906 he was awarded a civil list pension of £100 per annum and George Bernard Shaw did what he could to help him financially. However other issues were also circling besides poverty. Ill-health, and his declining intellectual powers, amplified by the onset of cancer, caused profound hopelessness and clinical depression.

Late in 1908, Davidson left London to live in Penzance in Cornwall. On 23rd March 1909, he left his house and was not seen again. There seemed no sound reason not to believe that he had done so with the intention of drowning himself. On an examination of his office a new manuscript was found. It was a poetry book; 'Fleet Street Poems', with a letter bleakly stating confirming, "This will be my last book."

Indeed in his philosophic book 'The Testament of John Davidson', published the year before his death, he anticipates this fate:

"None should outlive his power. . . . Who kills
Himself subdues the conqueror of kings;
Exempt from death is he who takes his life;
My time has come."

Davidson's body was not discovered until 18th September in Mount's cave by some fishermen. In accordance with his will it was now buried at sea. Strangely it seemed Davidson's wish that none of his unpublished works, nor any biography be published and "no word except of my writing is ever to appear in any book of mine as long as the copyright endures."

Davidson's poetry was a key early influence on important Modernist poets, in particular, his compatriot Hugh MacDiarmid, Wallace Stevens and T.S. Eliot.

John Davidson – A Concise Bibliography

The North Wall (1885)
Diabolus Amans (1885) Verse drama
Bruce (1886) A drama in five acts
Smith (1888) A tragedy
An Unhistorical Pastoral, A Romantic Farce (1889)
Scaramouch in Naxos (1889)
Perfervid: The Career of Ninian Jamieson (1890) with 23 Original Illustrations by Harry Furniss
The Great Men, And a Practical Novelist (1891) Illustrated by E. J. Ellis.
In a Music Hall, and other Poems (1891)
Laura Ruthven's Widowhood (with C. J. Wills) (1892)
Fleet Street Eclogues (1893)
The Knight of the Maypole, (1903)
Sentences and Paragraphs (1893)
Ballads and Songs (1894)
Baptist Lake (1894)
A Random Itinerary (1894)
A Full and True Account of the Wonderful Mission of Earl Lavender (1895)
St. George's Day (1895)
Fleet Street Eclogues (Second Series) (1896)
Miss Armstrong's and Other Circumstances (1896)
The Pilgrimage of Strongsoul and Other Stories (1896)
New Ballads (1897)
Godfrida, a play (1898)
The Last Ballad (1899)
Self's the Man, A tragi-comedy (1901)
The Testament of a Man Forbid (1901)
The Testament of a Vivisector (1901)
The Testament of an Empire Builder (1902)
A Rosary (1903)
The Knight of the Maypole: A Comedy in Four Acts (1903)
The Testament of a Prime Minister (1904)
The Ballad of a Nun (1905)
The Theatrocrat: A Tragic Play of Church and State (1905)
Holiday and other poems, with a note on poetry (1906)
The Triumph of Mammon (1907)
Mammon and His Message (1908)
The Testament of John Davidson (1908)
Fleet Street and other Poems, (1909)
Contributor to The Yellow Book

Montesquieu's Lettres Persanes (Persian Letters) (1892)
François Coppée's Pour la couronne (For the Crown) (1896)
Victor Hugo's Ruy Blas (A Queen's Romance) (1904)